FARM ANIMALS
TURKEY

Katie Dicker

A+
Smart Apple Media

Published by Smart Apple Media,
an imprint of Black Rabbit Books
P.O. Box 3263, Mankato, Minnesota, 56002
www.blackrabbitbooks.com

Printed in the United States of America,
at Corporate Graphics in North Mankato, Minnesota.

Designed by Hel James
Edited by Mary-Jane Wilkins

Library of Congress Cataloging-in-Publication Data

Dicker, Katie.
 Turkey / Katie Dicker.
     p. cm. -- (Farm animals)
 Includes bibliographical references and index.
 ISBN 978-1-62588-025-3
 1. Turkeys--Juvenile literature. I. Title.
 SF507.D53 2014
 636.5'92--dc23
                            2013000063

Feb 14
J

Photo acknowledgements
l = left, r = right, t = top, b = bottom
title page tristan tan/Shutterstock; 3, 4 iStockphoto/Thinkstock;
5 Richard Mann/Shutterstock; 6 iStockphoto/Thinkstock; 7 Hemera/
Thinkstock; 8 iStockphoto/Thinkstock; 9 OneSmallSquare/Shutterstock;
10 Jeff Banke/Shutterstock; 11, 12, 13 iStockphoto/Thinkstock;
14 Alexandr Vlassyuk/Shutterstock; 15 almondd/Shutterstock;
16 TonLammerts/Shutterstock; 17 iStockphoto/Thinkstock;
18 Bochkarev Photography/Shutterstock; 19 iStockphoto/Thinkstock;
20t grafvision, bl Nigel Paul Monckton/both Shutterstock, r iStockphoto/
Thinkstock; 21t iStockphoto/Thinkstock, r Amy McNabb, b ODM Studio/
both Shutterstock; 22 both iStockphoto/Thinkstock; 23 Im Perfect
Lazybones/Shutterstock
Cover Gelpi/Shutterstock

DAD0507
052013
9 8 7 6 5 4 3 2 1

Contents

My World

I am a turkey. I live on a farm
with lots of other turkeys.

Gobble!

Here are some of my flock.
We like to live outside, but we go indoors
at night to stay safe and sheltered.

**Turkeys need
a shelter to stay safe
from animals such as
snakes and owls.**

Head to Toe

I have a hard, pointed beak to scoop up food and water. A flap of skin called a snood hangs over it.

The flap of skin under my chin is called a wattle.

Wiggle

Our feathers keep us warm and dry.
We ruffle our feathers in the dirt
to keep our skin healthy.

Flap!

Most turkeys are too
heavy to be able to fly.

Turkey feathers are
usually white, gray,
brown, or black.

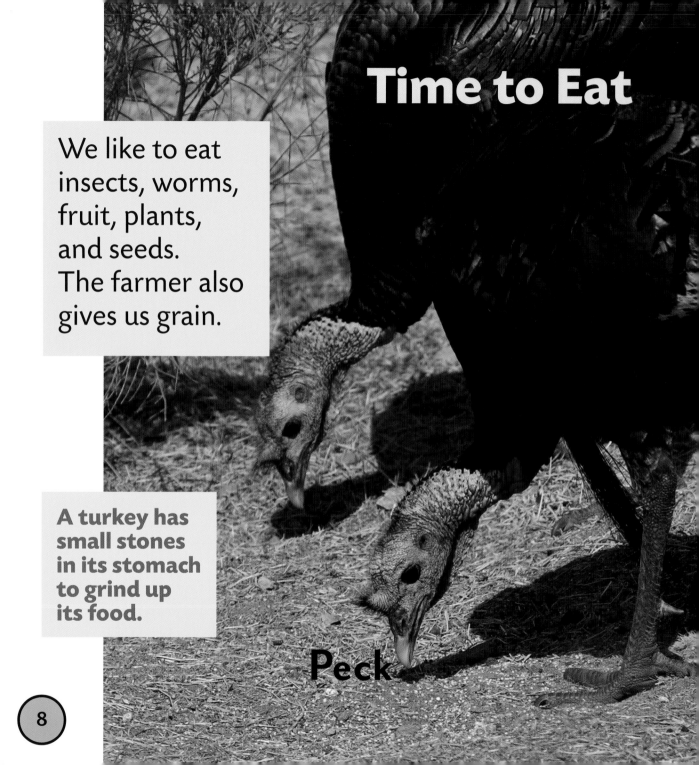

Time to Eat

We like to eat insects, worms, fruit, plants, and seeds. The farmer also gives us grain.

A turkey has small stones in its stomach to grind up its food.

Peck

We use our sharp claws to scratch the ground. Sometimes we find slugs and snails!

Fine Feathers

A male turkey is sometimes called a tom or a gobbler. He has a large wattle and snood.

The long, thin, dark feathers on a tom's chest are called a beard.

When males want to attract a female turkey, they puff up their feathers and fan their tails.

Male turkeys have more colorful feathers than females.

Sights and Sounds

I have no feathers on my head or neck. My skin changes color when I'm angry or excited.

A turkey's skin color can change from gray to shades of red, white, and blue.

12

Cluck!

Turkeys like to live in groups. They gobble, cluck, and cackle to show how they feel.

13

Baby Turkeys

Baby turkeys are called poults. A male poult is called a jake, and a female poult is called a jenny.

Baby turkeys hatch from an egg. They take about a month to hatch.

A female turkey can lay up to 18 eggs at a time. She sits on her eggs to keep them warm.

When baby turkeys hatch, their mother teaches them how to eat and drink.

Who Looks After Us?

The farmer gives us fresh straw and hay to keep our shelter clean and dry.

A visit from the vet also helps to keep us healthy.

The farmer checks our shelter is warm. Sometimes, farmers use heat lamps to keep us cozy.

Baby turkeys love to feel warmth on their feathers.

Farm Produce

Turkeys are farmed for their meat. People often eat roast turkey at Christmas, or during festivals such as Thanksgiving.

Big turkeys are good for feeding large groups of family and friends!

Turkeys can grow very quickly. When they reach a healthy weight, the farmer takes them to market.

More than 45 million turkeys are eaten in the US at Thanksgiving every year.

Turkeys Around the World

Red Ardennes, France

Farmers in countries all over the world keep turkeys. Some turkeys live in the wild. Here are some of the different breeds.

Royal Palm, USA

Bronze, USA and Europe

Wild, USA

Bourbon Red, USA

Ocellated, Mexico

Turkeys are native to the US. Europeans took them home in the 1500s, and now they are farmed all over the world.

Did You Know?

Turkeys can eat a lot and grow very quickly. They can put on a pound a week.

In the wild, turkeys live for about ten years.

Turkey eggs are bigger than chicken eggs. They are usually tan colored with brown speckles.

The largest farmed turkey weighed 86 pounds. That's big enough to feed more than 50 people!

Useful Words

flock
A group of turkeys that live together. A group can also be called a rafter.

grain
A type of cereal used for animal feed.

hatch
A baby turkey hatches when it comes out of its egg.

vet
A doctor who takes care of animals.

Index

beak 6
breeds 20, 21

claws 9

eggs 14, 15, 23

feathers 7, 10, 11, 12, 17
food 6, 8, 9, 15, 22

poults 14, 15, 17

shelter 5, 16, 17
skin 6, 7, 12
snood 6, 10

tail 11

wattle 6, 10

Web Links

www.kiddyhouse.com/Farm/Turkeys
www.facts-about.org.uk/facts-about-turkeys.htm
www.kidzone.ws/animals/turkey.htm
www.kidsfarm.com/turkeys.htm
www.ncagr.gov/cyber/kidswrld/general/barnyard/poultry.htm